Poetry Time
With
Dr. Seuss Rhyme

Cheryl Potts

Alleyside Press®

Fort Atkinson, Wisconsin

Also by Cheryl Potts

Poetry Galore and More With Shel Silverstein
Poetry Fun by the Ton With Jack Prelutsky

Published by Alleyside Press, an imprint of Highsmith Press
Highsmith Press
W5527 Highway 106
P.O. Box 800
Fort Atkinson, Wisconsin 53538-0800
1-800-558-2110

© Cheryl Potts, 1997
Cover design: Bill Higby

The paper used in this publication meets the minimum requirements of American National Standard for Information Science — Permanence of Paper for Printed Library Material. ANSI/NISO Z39.48-1992.

Library of Congress Cataloging-in-Publication Data
    Potts, Cheryl, 1953-
        Poetry time with Dr. Seuss rhyme / Cheryl Potts.
            p.   cm.
        Includes bibliographical references (p.)
        ISBN 0-917846-99-0 (alk. paper)
        1. Language arts (Elementary) 2. Poetry--Study and teaching
    (Elementary) 3. Education, Elementary--Activity programs.
    4. Seuss, Dr. I. Seuss, Dr. II. Title.
    LB1576.P684 1997
    372.6--DC21   97-31434
                                                            CIP

Contents

Introduction

Each year, elementary teachers and librarians take on the challenge and the awesome responsibility of teaching children how to read. This goes hand in hand with the pleasure of directing students to age-appropriate, quality and stimulating literature that will produce in them a lifelong desire to learn and read for enjoyment. We have also become self-esteem builders, motivators, and at times, attitude changers of children. These challenges create an ever present demand for innovative ideas and enthusiasm-building activities to keep our students on task.

Poetry Time With Dr. Seuss Rhyme was created for the elementary teacher or librarian who has embraced this task and become actively involved in the learning process of his or her students. This book was designed to create enthusiasm and excitement in the rhyme and rhythm of literature, as well as to reinforce early reading and language skills. To enhance student learning and curiosity, reserve a bulletin board and display table for a Seuss Center in the corner of your classroom, *(described on p. 7).*

For teacher convenience and usability, *Poetry Time With Dr. Seuss* has been divided into two sections: Primary Activities (K–2) and Intermediate Activities (3–5). The book encompasses a wide assortment of games, projects and activities using Dr. Seuss's imaginative books. Many of the games and activities can be adapted to fit your grade-level skill needs. These activities may also be used as evaluative tools for assessing student progress.

This author study creates springboards for many classroom activities using the appeal of Seuss's clever, silly characters to motivate children to read. Whenever possible literature links have been provided for each activity to extend further reading or research enjoyment. Culminating activities have been included at books end to tie up and complete the Dr. Seuss author study on a creative note. For further information on Dr. Seuss's many books, a bibliography has been provided as well as a teacher resource book list.

About Dr. Seuss

Theodor Seuss Geisel, better known as Dr. Seuss, has entertained children and adults with his imaginative characters and stories for more than 50 years.

Born March 2, 1904, in Springfield, Massachusetts, to Theodore Robert and Henrietta (Seuss) Geisel, he learned very early about the importance of seeking perfection. As a child, young Ted loved to draw and write funny stories. Though his high school art teacher told him he would never learn to draw, he pursued his art career with the encouragement and support of his future wife Helen Palmer. Geisel graduated from Dartmouth College in 1925 and studied briefly at Oxford. In 1927 he married Helen, returned to New York and began a fifteen-year period of creating advertising art and cartoons for magazines, newspapers and billboards. During this time he wrote and illustrated his first children's book, but it met with many rejections. Publishers insisted it wouldn't sell. However, in 1937, Vanguard Press decided to take a chance on *And to Think That I Saw It on Mulberry Street.* It became an instant success. It was with this book that he introduced his pseudonym, Dr. Seuss. He said, "I adopted this title to please my parents who had always hoped I'd become a medical doctor. But I figured I saved them about $10,000!" In 1956, Dartmouth presented him with an honorary doctorate degree, making his Dr. Seuss title official.

Book after book followed until, twenty years into his writing career, he, like many others at the time, was influenced by a single magazine article. In response to a 1954 *Life* article by John Hersey, "Why Do Students Bog Down on The First R?" Geisel wrote a book for beginning readers using fewer than 220 words. His book *The Cat in the Hat,* published in 1957, became the first in a series of Random House Beginner Books with comic rhymed texts and imaginative illustrations that would revolutionize reading. Geisel became president of Random House's Beginner Books division in 1958, where he would remain active up to the time of his death. He created thirteen more beginning readers, as well as writing several more books outside the series, his most recent in 1990.

On September 25, 1991, Theodor Seuss Geisel died peacefully at his home in La Jolla, California. He was 87 years old. Geisel is the author of 48 children's books that together have sold more than 200 million copies and have been translated into twenty languages.

During his career, Geisel won three Academy Awards, the Laura Ingalls Wilder Award in 1980 for making "a substantial and lasting contribution to literature for children," and the Pulitzer Prize in 1984 "for his contribution over nearly half a century to the education and enjoyment of America's children and their parents."

For more information about Dr. Seuss see the bibliography on p. 62.

Seuss Center

Create a Seuss Center in your classroom near a bulletin board. Display posters, pictures, book lists, bookmarks, etc. that promote Dr. Seuss books. By adding a small table under the bulletin board you can stand up various Dr. Seuss books for students to browse through and read. If possible, stock a small bookshelf with art supplies and materials for students to work on games, activities and projects that are described throughout the book. Check below for more supply and material suggestions for your Seuss Center.

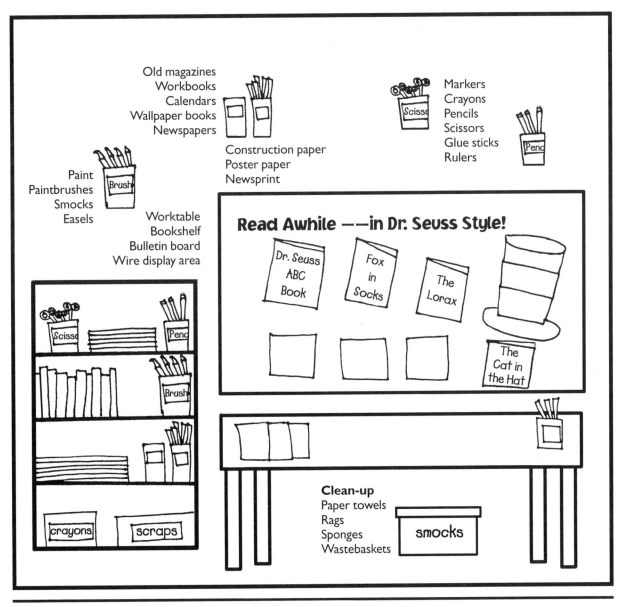

Old magazines
Workbooks
Calendars
Wallpaper books
Newspapers

Construction paper
Poster paper
Newsprint

Markers
Crayons
Pencils
Scissors
Glue sticks
Rulers

Paint
Paintbrushes
Smocks
Easels

Worktable
Bookshelf
Bulletin board
Wire display area

Read Awhile ——in Dr. Seuss Style!

Dr. Seuss ABC Book

Fox in Socks

The Lorax

The Cat in the Hat

Clean-up
Paper towels
Rags
Sponges
Wastebaskets

smocks

Activity One

Letter Recognition

As kindergarten children are introduced to alphabet letters and sounds, *Dr. Seuss's ABC* is a wonderful tool to get the excitement rolling. The zany creatures and colorful pages provide stimulation for our youngest learners to move into reading readiness.

ABC book display

Provide opportunities for students to enjoy other ABC books. Set up a permanent classroom learning center with a large ABC book display. Equip the center with magnetic letters and magnetic board, alphabet stencils, magna doodle board, pipe cleaners and plenty of paper and pencils. Students can manipulate magnetic letters and pipe cleaners (bending them to form letters), write with the magna doodle board and stencils and practice reading as they look at ABC books. This learning center should be an ongoing activity throughout the year.

Frog Jump game

To practice alphabet letter recognition, teach students how to play the Frog Jump game. This game is designed for whole group interaction. Ask students to sit in a circle around a hula hoop pond full of alphabet-lettered frogs. Each child gets a turn to "sneak up to the pond and grab a frog." The child must identify the letter (sound) to hang onto the frog and return to his/her place in the circle. If the child has difficulty, tell him/her the letter and say, "Oops, the frog jumped back into the pond. Try again." That same child has an opportunity to catch the same frog, repeating the letter again or choosing and correctly identifying a new letter frog. Thus, each child will return to the circle holding a frog.

To make the game, duplicate frog pattern on the next page. Label each frog with the capital and lowercase letter. Laminate the frogs for durability.

Cut & sort center

As students progress in alphabet recognition and sounds, provide some structured opportunities for them to reinforce those skills. Set up a cut and sort center with old workbooks or phonic worksheets. Children can practice cutting and sorting pictures according to the initial sounds. Label 26 white, business envelopes with a letter on each, placing them alphabetically in a sturdy box. Allow students to sort the pictures and place them in appropriate envelopes. These sorted pictures will be very useful in making games for your classroom.

Frog Jump pattern

Picture Wheel game

The Picture Wheel game is a perfect example of using the pre-sorted pictures as a learning tool. To create, use the circle patterns below. Using contrasting colors of construction paper cut out an equal number of large circles and small circles. On the small circles, make the triangular arrow black as shown. From your pre-sorted picture collection, choose workbook pictures of things that will help students to practice initial consonants and glue them to the center of each small circle.

To complete the large circles, write several consonant letters (no more than eight) around the circle edge. One of the letters must be the initial letter (sound) of the item in the picture on the small circle. Laminate these pieces and join at the center with a paper fastener.

To play, students line the arrow up with the initial letter of the item in the picture. To make this game self-correcting, place a black dot on the reverse side of the large circle behind the correct letter. Students can check themselves as they turn the picture wheel over. This game can be played by one to two players or as an independent skill check.

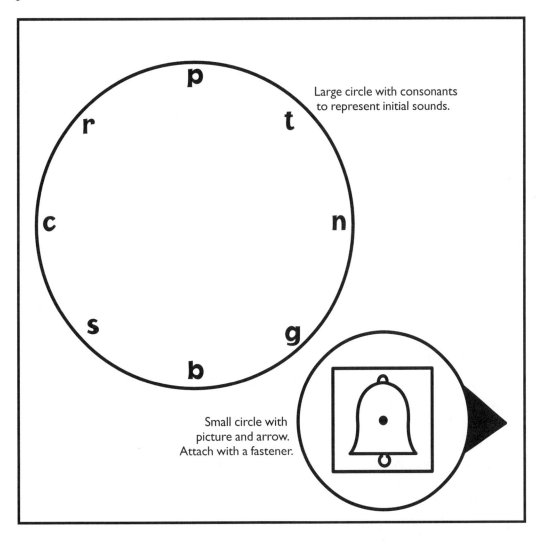

Large circle with consonants to represent initial sounds.

Small circle with picture and arrow. Attach with a fastener.

Book Making

As students review and enjoy the ABC book display in your classroom, invite them to gather ideas on creating an ABC book to share with other classrooms. This ABC book making activity would be especially appropriate for first and second graders as they write for a real audience—kindergarten children. This project may last over a period of time as kindergarten children study each letter of the alphabet or as an end of year wrap-up review.

Ask students to bring in magazines, old calendars, and junk mail (with pictures) for illustrating a collage-style book. The pre-sorted workbook pictures (Activity One) would also be useful in adding to the variety in size and type you need to create the collage effect.

To make an ABC big book, use 12" x 18" white construction paper—using the left-hand page for the text and the right-hand page for the letter-appropriate pictures. Using a format similar to the one introduced by Dr. Seuss, you could begin with the following: "BIG A, little a... What begins with Aa?" Allow the bottom of the page to remain blank. (After the ABC book is completed and laminated, picture names can be written in the blank area with a black marker during lesson time as you assist kindergarten students in letter and word writing practice.) If 1st and 2nd graders take on this activity as a special writing project to present to the kindergarten classroom, they may add the picture names on the text page for the kindergarten students to track visually as you read.

On the opposite page, students will glue and arrange cutout pictures in a collage. The letter Aa page may have pictures such as: apron, acorn, ant, arrow, angel, aspirin, antelope, anchor, apple, etc. *(See p.12 for sample book and additional ideas)*

To finish the ABC book, punch holes in the top, middle and bottom of each page and fasten the book together with loose-leaf rings.

Additional ABC books

The following ABC books will greatly enhance your classroom learning center: *Alphabatics* by Suse MacDonald (New York: Macmillan, 1992); *Animalia* by Graeme Base (New York: Willowisp Press, 1986); *Chicka Chicka Boom Boom* by Bill Martin, Jr. (New York: Simon & Schuster, 1989); *The Furry Alphabet Book* (1991) and *The Icky Bug Alphabet Book* by Jerry Pallotta (Watertown, MA: Charlesbridge, 1986); *Annie, Bea, and Chi Chi Dolores* by Donna Maurer (Boston: Houghton Mifflin, 1993); *Clifford's ABC* by Norman Bridwell (New York: Scholastic Inc., 1983); *The Elephant Alphabet Book* by Gene Yates (Chicago: Kidsbooks, 1995); *A,B, See!* by Tana Hoban (New York: Greenwillow, 1982); *A to Z* by Sandra Boynton (New York: Little Simon, 1990); *Alphabet Soup* by Kate Banks (New York: Knopf, 1988); *Alphabet Tree* by Leo Lionni (New York: Knopf, 1990); and *Alphabears: An ABC Book* by Kathleen Hague (New York: Henry Holt, 1984).

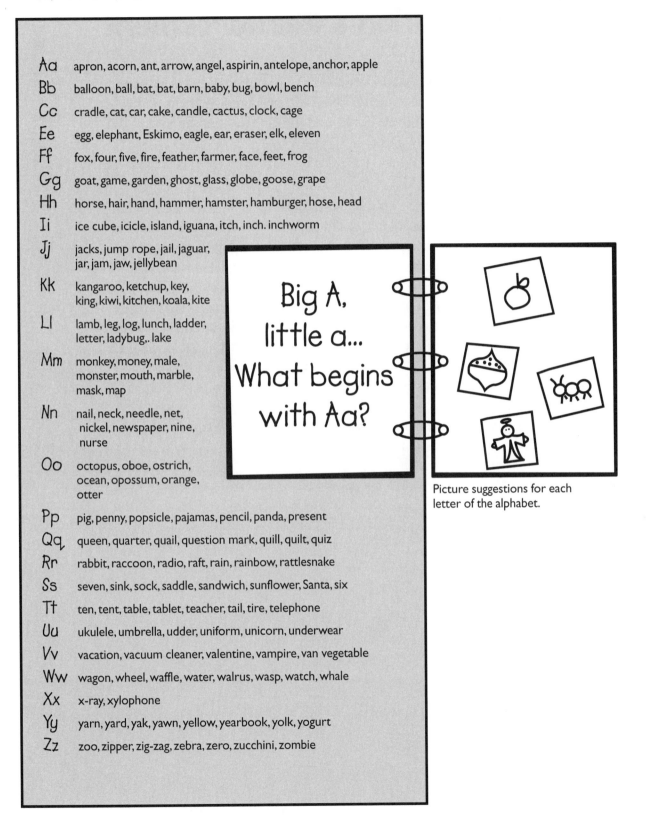

Aa	apron, acorn, ant, arrow, angel, aspirin, antelope, anchor, apple
Bb	balloon, ball, bat, bat, barn, baby, bug, bowl, bench
Cc	cradle, cat, car, cake, candle, cactus, clock, cage
Ee	egg, elephant, Eskimo, eagle, ear, eraser, elk, eleven
Ff	fox, four, five, fire, feather, farmer, face, feet, frog
Gg	goat, game, garden, ghost, glass, globe, goose, grape
Hh	horse, hair, hand, hammer, hamster, hamburger, hose, head
Ii	ice cube, icicle, island, iguana, itch. inchworm
Jj	jacks, jump rope, jail, jaguar, jar, jam, jaw, jellybean
Kk	kangaroo, ketchup, key, king, kiwi, kitchen, koala, kite
Ll	lamb, leg, log, lunch, ladder, letter, ladybug,. lake
Mm	monkey, money, male, monster, mouth, marble, mask, map
Nn	nail, neck, needle, net, nickel, newspaper, nine, nurse
Oo	octopus, oboe, ostrich, ocean, opossum, orange, otter
Pp	pig, penny, popsicle, pajamas, pencil, panda, present
Qq	queen, quarter, quail, question mark, quill, quilt, quiz
Rr	rabbit, raccoon, radio, raft, rain, rainbow, rattlesnake
Ss	seven, sink, sock, saddle, sandwich, sunflower, Santa, six
Tt	ten, tent, table, tablet, teacher, tail, tire, telephone
Uu	ukulele, umbrella, udder, uniform, unicorn, underwear
Vv	vacation, vacuum cleaner, valentine, vampire, van vegetable
Ww	wagon, wheel, waffle, water, walrus, wasp, watch, whale
Xx	x-ray, xylophone
Yy	yarn, yard, yak, yawn, yellow, yearbook, yolk, yogurt
Zz	zoo, zipper, zig-zag, zebra, zero, zucchini, zombie

Big A, little a... What begins with Aa?

Picture suggestions for each letter of the alphabet.

Color Recognition & Reinforcement

A good snowy day, when students are overjoyed and bubbling with excitement is the time to read *How the Grinch Stole Christmas!* After discussing the mounds of snow mushrooming over the Whoville homes and the Grinch's poor dog Max you might play this color recognition game.

Blizzard

Use the pattern on the next page duplicate enough snowflakes so that each child will have one. Color each a single color and add the color word in the center of the flake. Color the snowflakes purple, yellow, green, red, brown, black, blue, orange, pink and white. Or you may wish to involve your children in coloring and cutting out the snowflakes. When you're finished, laminate them for durability.

To play the game, ask children to sit in a circle. Pass out one snowflake to each child, making sure that each color is used more than once. Tell students that when you call a color, those children (two or more) have to get up and change places with another child who is holding a snowflake of the same color as quickly as possible. You may call two colors at a time to heighten the fun. But when you say "Blizzard," *everyone* must get up and change places, quickly and carefully.

Another story link to read before playing this game is ***The Snowy Day*** by Ezra Jack Keats (New York: Scholastic Inc., 1962).

Sorting

Clothing Sort game

The Clothing Sort game is for kindergarten children. Using 5" x 8" index cards, paste a picture or drawing of an article of hot or cold weather clothing on each. Label the cards and laminate for durability. Make two headbands, one with a picture of the sun on it and one with a picture of a snowflake. Designate two children to be the leaders and wear the headbands. Pass out the clothing cards, one per child, making sure the children know what their picture is.

Instruct students to look at their clothing cards and decide which leader they should stand behind. Note how quickly children can figure out where they belong. Discuss proper outer wear for different temperatures and weather conditions (rainy, fall).

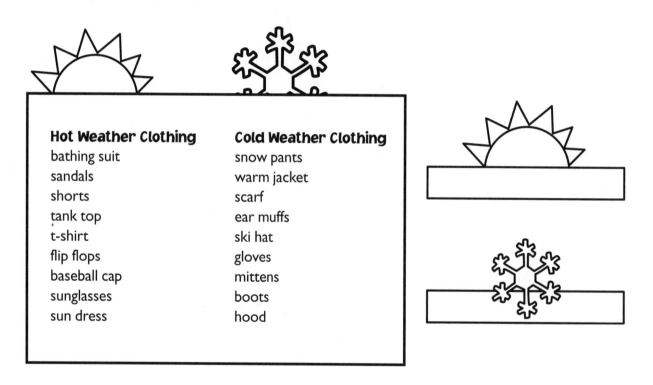

Hot Weather Clothing	Cold Weather Clothing
bathing suit	snow pants
sandals	warm jacket
shorts	scarf
tank top	ear muffs
t-shirt	ski hat
flip flops	gloves
baseball cap	mittens
sunglasses	boots
sun dress	hood

Comical books to read to your students after this game are *Thomas's Snowsuit* by Robert Munsch (Toronto: Annick Press, 1985) and *Mrs. Toggle's Zipper* by Robin Pulver (New York: Scholastic Inc., 1990).

Descriptive Words & Adjectives

After reading the Grinch story, ask your students to brainstorm and list (on chart paper) words that describe the Grinch's personality and behavior, for example: nasty, mean, unkind, cheater, greedy, hater, sour, snarly, growler, scary, trickster, liar, and unhappy. On a separate piece of chart paper, write the name "Grinch" vertically in large letters. You may wish to draw a picture of the Grinch in the background. Make a word puzzle using the descriptive words that the students listed. This chart may be done together, filling and fitting in the words using the letters in the "Grinch" name as an acrostic. For older students, you may wish to assign this as an independent activity after your specific instructions.

Description & Attributes

After reading *How the Grinch Stole Christmas!*, discuss the Christmas traditions of the people in Who-ville, comparing them to your own family traditions: waking up bright and early, rushing to the tree to search for presents, sitting down to a big dinner, singing Christmas songs. Notice the similarities. The Grinch couldn't stand all the Who-ville festivities. Further discuss how the Grinch made a startling turnaround in his attitude.

Guess the Gift game

Two weeks before Christmas, ask your students to share what they would like for Christmas. List these items on chart paper decorated for the holidays. Then enlarge and pass out a copy of the gift pattern below. Have students write one present they would like to get for Christmas on the back of the gift pattern. On the front of the gift pattern, they must describe the gift without saying what it is. Suggest to students that they might describe what the gift looks like or how it smells. Finish up by having students color and cut out the gift boxes. Then collect all the gifts and place them in a box. Mix them up.

To play Guess the Gift, choose a gift from the box, read the description and ask students to "guess the gift" (by raising their hand). The first student to guess correctly holds the gift. Students may not guess when their own gift is drawn. Play continues until the children guess all the gifts. The student with the most gifts at the end of the game chooses a gift from the treasure box or other appropriate prize.

A great book to read before or after playing Guess the Gift is *The Very Best Christmas Present* by Jim Razzi (New York: Western, 1988.)

Holiday Songs

After reading the Grinch story, discuss the various holiday traditions that families celebrate. Even the Whos of Whoville had traditions! One tradition was, "they'd stand hand-in-hand and SING! SING! SING!" Perhaps the Whos had special Christmas carols. Ask students to imagine themselves as a member of Whoville and compose a Christmas carol. To get students started on their own creative songs, ask them to list words or phrases centered around Christmas celebrations. For example: making cookies, frosting, candy canes, stars, icicles, lights, trimming the tree, etc. Then ask them to think of some familiar children's songs. Such as: "ABC Song," "BINGO," "Farmer in the Dell," "Ten Little Indians," "Pop Goes the Weasel," etc. Students then fit the words, phrases and sentences to the rhythm of the familiar tunes. Display these student creations around the room or put them together on loose leaf rings and display them on a chart holder for children to flip through. Here are a few tunes with new holiday lyrics I created:

Christmas Tree
(Sung to the tune of "Twinkle, Twinkle Little Star")

Twinkle, twinkle, Christmas tree
Watch the tree lights blink at me.
Tinsel sparkles everywhere
On my socks and in my hair.
Twinkle, twinkle, what a sight!
Santa's coming here tonight.

Little Snowman
(Sung to the tune of "I'm a Little Teapot")

I'm a little snowman wearing clothes.
Here is my scarf and carrot nose.
When you get me dressed up I will say,
"Put on my boots so I can play!"

Dear Santa
(Sung to the tune of "Mary Had a Little Lamb")

Dear Santa, I have made a list,
Made a list, made a list.
Santa I have made a list.
It's longer than last year's.

I'd like a box of building blocks,
Building blocks, building blocks.
I'd like a treasure chest that locks
And race car I can steer.

I'd like train set and a track,
Silly putty, baseball hat,
A hundred packs of baseball cards,
And headphones for my ears.

Dear Santa, I have made a list,
Made a list, made a list.
Santa, could you bring all this?
Just add a new reindeer!

My Christmas List
Building Blocks
Treasure Chest
Race Car
Train Set
Silly Putty
Baseball Hat
Baseball Cards
Headphones

Ten Little Snowflakes

You may wish to teach your students the song "Frosty the Snowman" or read *Frosty the Snowman* by Annie North Bedford (New York: Golden Book, 1950).

Using the snowflake pattern on p. 15, copy, cut out and write a number from one to ten on each snowflake, then laminate. Choose ten children to hold the snowflakes and have them stand when their number is sung. Use the following song to the tune of "Ten Little Indians."

1 little, 2 little, 3 little snowflakes,
4 little, 5 little, 6 little snowflakes,
7 little, 8 little, 9 little snowflakes,
10 little snowflakes fall.

Ask the children to stand with their snowflakes. As the class sings, have the children raise their snowflakes above their heads when their number is sung. Then have them all let go of their snowflakes together when the class sings the word "fall."

Sing That Tune

For a musical sequencing game or as part of your holiday party celebrations, divide your class in half to play Sing That Tune. First, write two to three words or short phrases on single 3"x 5" cards using the chorus from "Jingle Bells" and the first verse of "Deck the Halls." Mix up the cards. Designate one side of the room to be the "Jingle Bells" side and the opposite side to be the "Deck the Halls" side. Then pass out a 3"x 5" card to each student. Students are to read the card, move to the correct side of the room, work together and arrange themselves in the right order. The group who is finished first, starts singing their song. For an amusing variation, each student must sing his/her word or phrase only, then turn to the next student to sing their words, all the way down the line.

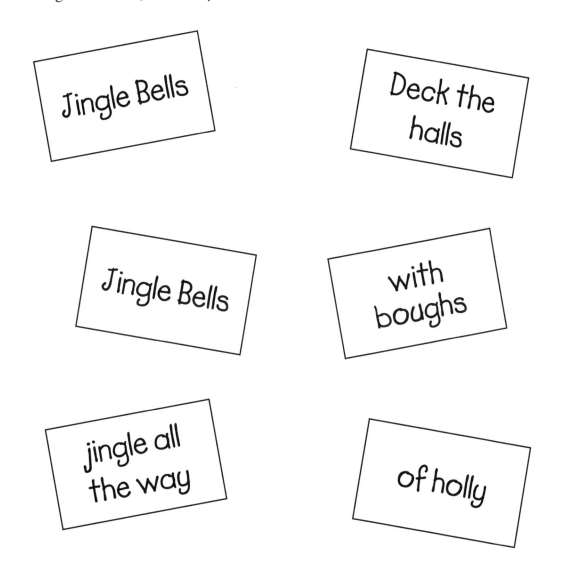

For additional Christmas songs and poetry, enjoy the book and tape of *It's Christmas* by Jack Prelutsky (New York: Scholastic Inc., 1981) or *Holiday Piggyback Songs* compiled by Jean Warren (Everett, WA: Warren, 1988)

 **Activity Eight**

Christmas Skill Cards

During December when classroom excitement and noise levels are at an all-time high, learning seems to take a beating (or so we think). Inform your students that there will be small group and individual "quiet" work stations (or centers) that will be used when regular morning and group time activities are finished. Arrange your classroom to accommodate a rectangular table where (up to four) children can work on Christmas tree ornaments. Display a finished ornament, supplies and direction sheet for small group, quiet work time. *(You may wish to change the ornament project each week for variety.)*

Another work station area is defined by a clothesline strung across the classroom to display the Christmas skill cards. Clothespins work well for clipping cards to the line. Allow students to choose one Christmas skill card at a time off the line (pull gently), pick up a skill card sheet (sample below) to record answers, then work quietly at their own desk. Instruct students to locate the Christmas skill card number and write it on the sheet along with their name and the date. Remind them to place the finished skill card sheet on your desk and clip the Christmas skill card back up on the line (if they can reach it). Inform them that a job well done earns them extra credit points, a pick from the candy jar, a free homework pass, extra play time, extra time at the tree ornament table, or any other grade-level appropriate reward.

Well in advance, use teacher aides, parent volunteers or older students to help prepare the Christmas skill cards. If done well the first time and laminated, they will last for years! Dig out or purchase Christmas bulletin board pictures, old calendars, *Ideal* magazines, and coloring books that have eye appeal to your students. Use the overhead projector or copy machine to enlarge drawings. The pictures and skill ideas on the following pages may inspire some ideas of your own. See p. 28 for answers to the skills activities.

Christmas Skill Card Sheet

Name _____

Date _____ Card Number _____

Blank worksheets can be available for students when they have time to work on the Skills Cards.

1.

List as many adjectives as you can to describe how you would feel if you saw Santa at your house on Christmas Eve.
(example: excited)

2.

Illustrate 5 of these words:
1. wreath
2. package
3. mistletoe
4. candle
5. stocking
6. ornaments
7. sleigh
8. caroling
9. reindeer
10. feast
11. candy canes
12. sledding
13. Santa
15. North Pole
16. Christmas Eve
17. cookies
17. Christmas Tree
18. fireplace
19. Christmas morning
20. Holiday fun

3.

List as many Christmas or Wintertime compound words as you can.
(examples: reindeer, snowball)

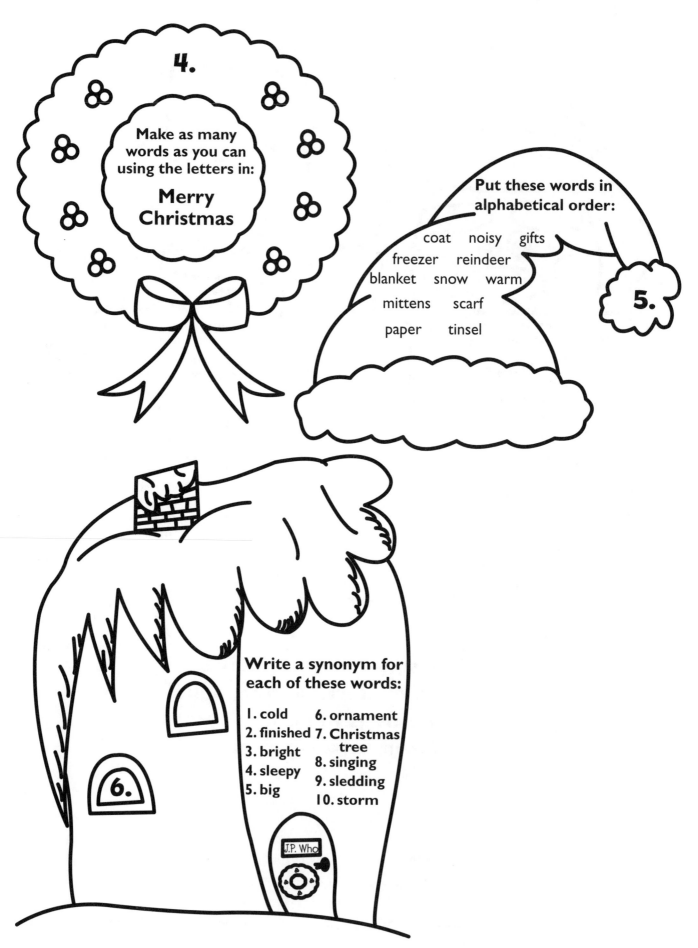

4.

Make as many words as you can using the letters in:

Merry Christmas

Put these words in alphabetical order:

coat   noisy   gifts

freezer   reindeer

blanket   snow   warm

mittens   scarf

paper   tinsel

5.

Write a synonym for each of these words:

1. cold
2. finished
3. bright
4. sleepy
5. big
6. ornament
7. Christmas tree
8. singing
9. sledding
10. storm

6.

J.P. Who

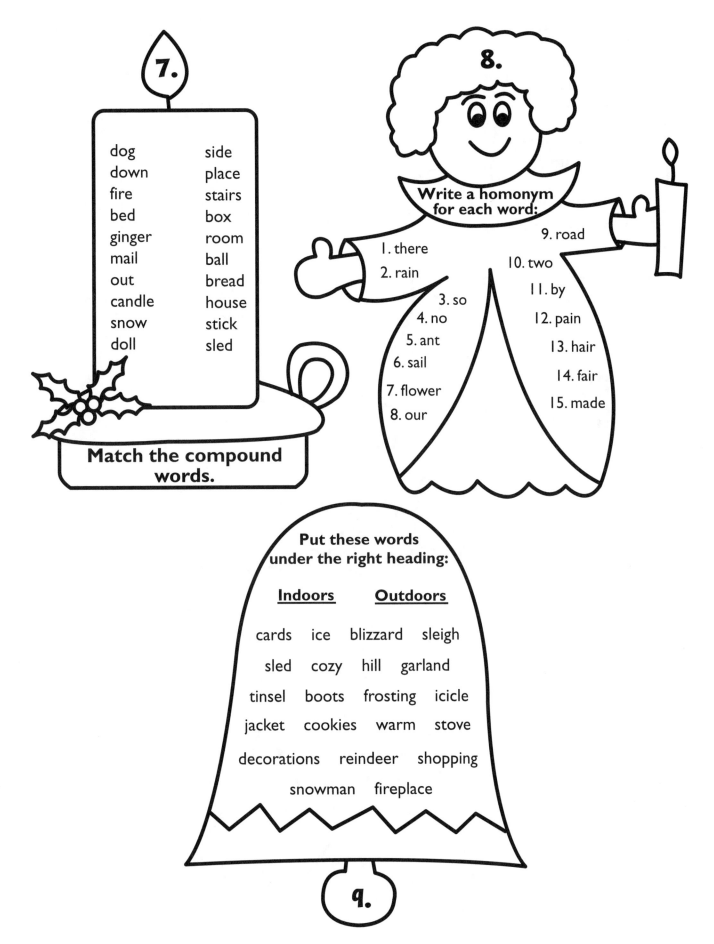

7.

dog   side
down   place
fire   stairs
bed   box
ginger room
mail   ball
out   bread
candle house
snow stick
doll   sled

Match the compound words.

8.

Write a homonym for each word:

1. there
2. rain
3. so
4. no
5. ant
6. sail
7. flower
8. our
9. road
10. two
11. by
12. pain
13. hair
14. fair
15. made

Put these words under the right heading:

__Indoors__   __Outdoors__

cards ice blizzard sleigh

sled cozy hill garland

tinsel boots frosting icicle

jacket cookies warm stove

decorations reindeer shopping

snowman fireplace

9.

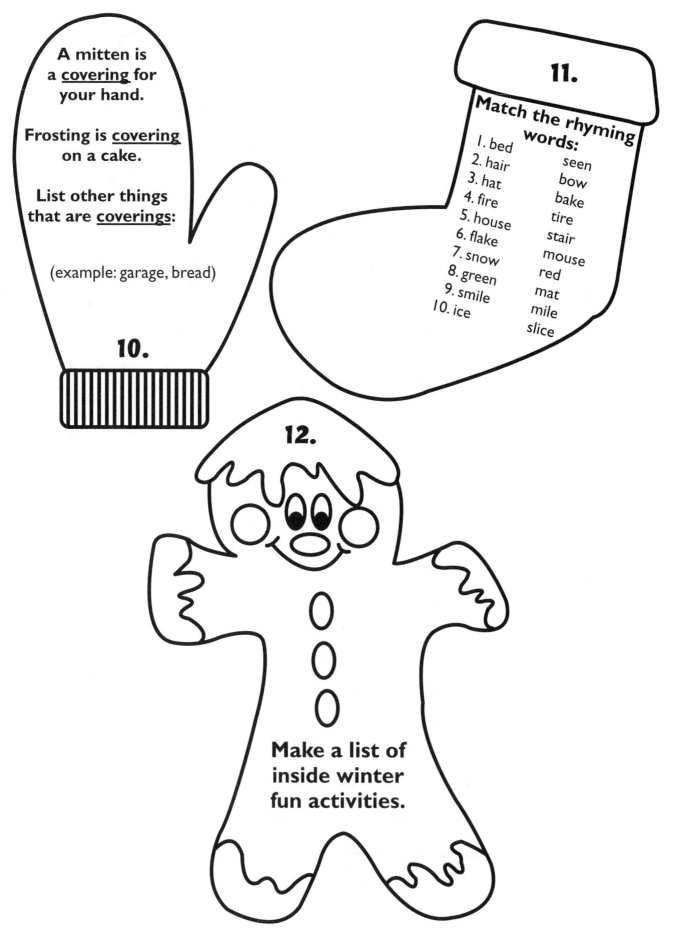

A mitten is a <u>covering</u> for your hand.

Frosting is <u>covering</u> on a cake.

List other things that are <u>coverings</u>:

(example: garage, bread)

10.

11.

Match the rhyming words:

1. bed
2. hair
3. hat
4. fire
5. house
6. flake
7. snow
8. green
9. smile
10. ice

seen
bow
bake
tire
stair
mouse
red
mat
mile
slice

12.

Make a list of inside winter fun activities.

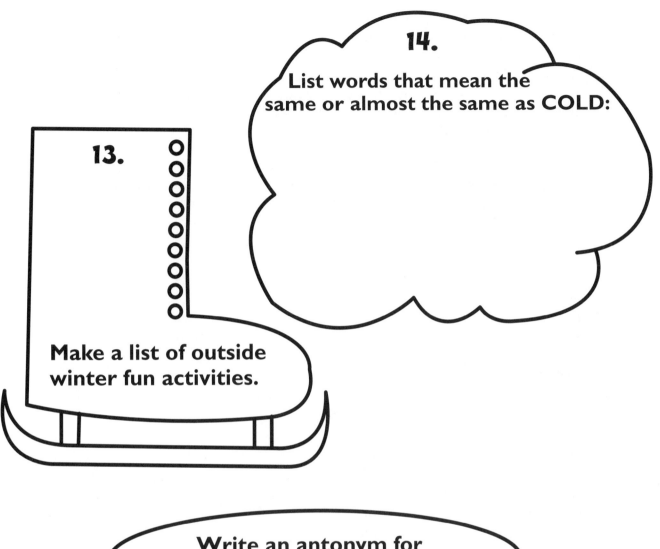

13.

Make a list of outside winter fun activities.

14.

List words that mean the same or almost the same as COLD:

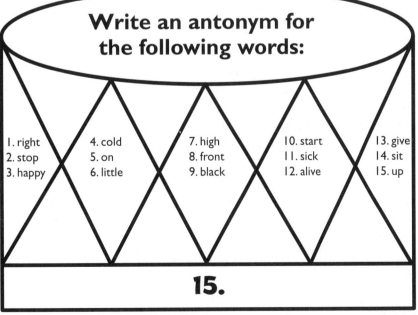

Write an antonym for the following words:

1. right
2. stop
3. happy
4. cold
5. on
6. little
7. high
8. front
9. black
10. start
11. sick
12. alive
13. give
14. sit
15. up

15.

Christmas Skill Cards Answer Key

For questions 1, 3–5, 10, and 12–15 the answers here are examples of possible correct answers. Accept any other correct answers also.

1. Excited, thrilled, happy, glad, fortunate, cheerful, amazed, delighted, joyful, enthralled, elated, exuberant.

2. Accept any illustration.

3. Snowman, snowplow, fireplace, showshoes, snowfall, marshmallow, sweetheart, mistletoe, mailbox, mailman, frostbite, snowsuit, snowpants, snowblower, snowdrift, popcorn, toyland, bedspread, backyard, rooftop, housetop, weekend, Sunday, cupcake, gingerbread, dollhouse, staircase, stairway, outside, inside, starlight.

4. I, a, is, it, am, as, at, are, his, miss, hiss, 'tis, sis, sit, hit, ham, ram, tam, yam, has, mass, mat, sat, hat, rat, cat, mare, care, fare, hare rare, tear, rear, hear, mast, cast, hairy, stir, her, far, sir, Mr., Mrs., cry, try, my, sty, tie, may, say, ray, hay, stay, tray, etc.

5. blanket, coat, freezer, gifts, mittens, noisy, paper, reindeer, scarf, snow, tinsel, warm.

6. 1. (freezing), 2. (done), 3. (shiny), 4. (tired), 5. (large), 6. (decoration) 7. (pine tree), 8. (caroling), 9. (sliding), 10. (blizzard).

7. dogsled, downstairs, fireplace, bedroom, gingerbread, mailbox, outside, candlestick, snowball, dollhouse.

8. 1. (their, they're), 2. (rein, reign), 3. (sew), 4. (know), 5. (aunt), 6. (sale), 7. (flour), 8. (hour), 9. (rode), 10. (to, too), 11. (buy, bye), 12. (pane), 13. (hare), 14. (fare), 15. (maid).

9.

Indoors	Outdoors
cards	ice
cozy	blizzard
garland	sleigh
tinsel	sled
frosting	hill
cookies	boots
warm	icicle
stove	jacket
decorations	decorations
shopping	reindeer
fireplace	snowman

10. sock, shoe, hat, umbrella, sunglasses, hair, eyelid, skin, earmuffs, mittens, gloves, scarf, snowsuit, curtain, quilt, blanket, sheets, pillowcase, rug, carpet, tablecloth, shade, doghouse, roof, lid, hood, Band-Aid, makeup, hat, wig, mask.

11. 1. (red), 2. (stair), 3. (mat), 4. (tire), 5. (mouse), 6. (bake), 7. (bow), 8. (seen), 9. (mile), 10. (slice).

12. Play a game, read books, draw picture, color, write stories, put on a puppet show, dress up, make crafts, make up songs, bake desserts, reorganize bedroom, write letters, send cards, make up rhymes, play card games.

13. Sledding, snowmobiling, ice fishing, playing King of the Mountain, tobogganing, skiing, snow boarding, snowball fight, building snowman, building snow fort, ice skating, making snow angels.

14. Frigid, chilly, cool, freezing, nippy, shivery, icy.

15. 1. (left, wrong), 2. (go), 3. (sad), 4. (hot), 5. (off), 6. (big), 7. (low), 8. (back), 9. (white), 10. (finish), 11. (well), 12. (dead), 13. (take), 14. (stand), 15. (down).

 Activity Nine

Verbs & Suffixes

After reading *The Foot Book*, list all the things feet can do on a chart:

walk kick swing grow sweat jog run skip slip jump swim climb flip dance slide

Ask students to choose a verb (an action word) to use in a sentence and to illustrate. For older students, instruct them to add the endings: -s, -ed, -ing, and -er to the verb they choose. Add these sentences to the root word sentence and illustrate.

If you choose to make this a class book, brainstorm and vote on a title, for example, "Foot Loose," "Footsie," "Busy Feet," "Funny Feet."

 Activity Ten

Nouns & Vocabulary Development

Using the illustrations and text of *The Foot Book*, brainstorm a list of things we can wear on our feet. This list could generate much discussion on new vocabulary words as well as similarities and differences between various types of footwear, for example:

socks, shoes, sneakers, boots, clogs, Paks, slippers, flip flops, sandals, buckle shoes, velcro shoes, waders, cleats, ballet slippers, mukluks.

Footwear Confusion

A fun outdoor activity called Footwear Confusion could be a culminating activity on this topic. Ask your students to form a circle, take two giant steps backward, then sit on the ground. Have students turn around, so their backs face the center of the circle. Instruct them to untie or unbuckle both of their shoes and throw them over their shoulders into the circle. Quickly push the shoes to the center of the circle, mixing and heaping them up. On the count of five, students are to get up, go to the center of the circle, find their shoes, go back to the edge of the circle and put them on. When a student has both shoes properly fastened, he or she stands up. For a competitive flair, compete with another classroom of students. Reward or cheer for the winners as appropriate.

For further reading on this topic, try *Whose Shoes Are These?* by Ron Roy (New York: Clarion, 1988).

Fine Motor Coordination

For kindergarten children learning how to tie, buckle or otherwise fasten shoes, make a "Shoe Board" as a learning center activity. Purchase some used but clean tie and velcro sneakers, buckle shoes and any other interesting or unique footwear from a thrift shop, choosing a variety of sizes. Arrange the footwear in different orientations on a piece of pine board, so three or four children could practice at a time. Either hot glue or nail the shoes in place. You may wish to paint or decorate the shoes with markers or paint. Allow students time to practice at the center throughout the day. If you want to recognize the children who master the skills of fastening footwear, decorate a bulletin board with pictures of different colored shoes. As students demonstrate their skills, write their name on a shoe, signifying their success. Use the shoes below as patterns.

Creative Writing & Rhyming

After reading *One Fish Two Fish Red Fish Blue Fish* discuss the different nonsense animals throughout the book. It contains many creatures involved in rhyming patterns:

> Mr. Gump owns a wump.
> > Ned has a little bed.
> > > Mike pushes the bike.
> A Nook can't read a book.
> > A Zans can open cans.
> > > A Gox who can box.
> A Ying likes to sing.
> > A Yink likes to drink.
> > > Zeds have one hair on their heads.
> Out back we play "Ring the Gack."
> > We found Clark in the park.
> > > We can sleep with our pet Zeep.

Ask your students to use their first, middle, last name, or a name of someone in their family, to create a nonsense animal that can do something that rhymes, for example:

My pet Smith likes to kith.
A little Potts has lots of spots.
Tiny Michelle can play a gold bell.

Sammy has a smelly friend Hammy.
The big red Tony is very boney.

After students create their nonsense creature rhymes ask them to illustrate each. Share these rhymes and pictures with the class.

Celebrate Seuss buttons

Now that your students have had an opportunity to make zany creatures and write rhyming verse in Dr. Seuss style, they can become "Dr. Seuss Associates" or "Students of Seuss." Design and wear buttons that "Celebrate Seuss" and encourage students to be imaginative and creative.

Counting & Number Words

Introduce your students to these counting books and poems to reinforce number and number word recognition: *One Hungry Monster* by Susan Heyboer O'Keefe (New York, Scholastic Inc., 1989), *The Crayon Counting Book* by Jerry and Ryan Pallotta and Pam Munoz (Watertown, MA: Charlesbridge, 1996), *The Right Number of Elephants* by Jeff Sheppard (New York: Scholastic Inc., 1990), *The Big Fat Hen* by Keith Baker (New York: Harcourt Brace, 1994), *"Countdown"* by Jack Prelutsky from *Reader's Digest Children's Book of Poetry* (Pleasantville, NY: Reader's Digest, 1992) and *"Ten Fingers"* from *Read Aloud Rhymes for the Very Young* (New York: Knopf, 1986).

Grab That Fish

To review number words, play Grab That Fish. Using the fish patterns below, write numbers and number words on the fish, using numbers one through twelve. Ask the children to color unique-looking fish. Laminate and cut out. To play, instruct children to sit in a circle on the carpet. Ask them to imagine that they are sitting on the edge of a fish pond. Spread the fish inside the circle. Each child may get a turn to grab a fish and identify the number or the word on the fish. If correct, they keep the fish; if not, they throw it back (after reinforcing the correct answer). The student with the most fish wins and gets a gummy worm or a certificate for a free fish sandwich at McDonald's.

Singular & Plural

After reading Dr. Seuss's egg books, discuss the concept of singular (one) and plural (more than one) forms of words. Several words from the egg books serve as examples for this activity. Make a chart with your students to aid them in the difficult task of singular to plural spelling changes. As you come across words in daily reading and writing activities, add them to your chart.

Singular	Plural -s	Plural -es	Plural -ies	Plural f to v -es	Plural same	Plural vowel change
car	cars					
book	books					
egg	eggs					
goat	goats					
house		houses				
box		boxes				
baby			babies			
party			parties			
family			families			
knife				knives		
half				halves		
fish					fish	
deer					deer	
mouse						mice
goose						geese

Presto-Chango

To reinforce singular and plural forms of words, create a puzzle match game called Presto-Chango. Using commercially purchased sentence strip paper, cut twenty strips down to 8" long. Label the left half of the strip with the singular form of a word, leaving room to draw or paste a picture of the word. Label the right half with the plural form. With a black marker, draw a zig-zagged line to indicate the cutting line for the puzzle. Laminate the strip, then cut along the zig-zagged line. Mix up the puzzle pieces for students to match together. Use this activity in small groups or as an evaluation tool for individual students.

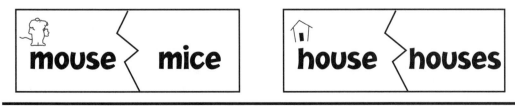

Edible activity

For an edible culminating activity, encourage your students to bring in a green snack to share. You may want to brainstorm a list of green foods: lime Jell-O, celery, lettuce, mint jelly, pickles, peppers, broccoli, peas, lime sherbet, avocado, kiwi, grapes, spinach, asparagus, cucumbers, zucchini.

You may wish to challenge your students to sing the following poems I have created for green foods as quickly as they can:

Green Foods
(Sung to the tune of "Ten Little Indians")

Celery, pickles, grapes, lime Jell-O,
Lettuce, spinach, avocados,
Broccoli, peas and moldy peaches.
All these foods are green.

Peppers, celery, pickles, kiwis,
Grapes and lettuce, spinach, peas,
Avocados and zucchinis.
All these foods are green.

For further reading

If you wish to follow the theme of green for kindergarten color week or St. Patrick's Day, use the books *Pickle Things* by Marc Brown (New York: Trumpet Club, 1980), *If You Walk Down This Road* by Kate Duke (New York: Trumpet Club, 1993), *Spring Green* by Valrie M. Selkowe (Lothrop, Lee & Shepard, 1985), *Frog and Toad Are Friends* by Arnold Lobel (New York: Harper Trophy, 1970), *The Very Hungry Caterpillar* by Eric Carle (New York: Philomel Books, 1987), *Turtle Tale* by Frank Asch (New York: Scholastic Inc., 1978), *Jump Frog Jump* by Robert Kalan (New York: Mulberry Books, 1981), *The Ants and the Grasshopper* by Kate Caton (Austin, TX: Steck-Vaughn, 1989), *Jog, Frog, Jog* by Barbara Gregorich (Grand Haven, MI: School Zone, 1992), *Tiny Timothy Turtle* by Anna Leditschke (Milwaukee, WI: Gareth Stevens, 1991), *Timothy Turtle* by Alice Vaught Davis (New York: Harcourt, 1940), *The St. Patrick's Day Shamrock Mystery* by Marion Markham (Boston: Houghton Mifflin, 1995), *Clever Tom and the Leprechaun* by Linda Shute (New York: Scholastic Inc., 1988) and *Mary McLean and the St. Patrick's Day Parade* by Steven Kroll (New York: Scholastic Inc., 1991).

Alphabetical Order

Using the egg pattern below, label the eggs with the name of a bird character from the *Scrambled Eggs Super!* Ask students to put these bird eggs in ABC order. Since there are 26 bird characters, you may want to divide them up between two groups of students. For a competitive activity, see which group finishes first.

The 26 bird characters characters are: Hen, Ruffle-Necked Sal-ma-goox, Tizzle-Topped Grouse, Mop-Noodled Finch, Beagle-Beaked Bald-Headed Grinch, Shade Roosting Quail, Lass-a-Lack's Tail, Spritz, Flannel-Wing Jay, Twiddler Owls, Kweet, Stroodel, Kwigger, Long-Legger Kwong, Grice, Pelf, Singl-File Zummzian Zuks, Mr. Stookoo Cuckoo, Tizzy, South-West-Facing Cranes, Grickily Gractus, Ziffs, Zuffs, Moth-Watching Sneth, Dawf, Bombastic Aghast.

Egg pattern

Bird research projects

For older students, this would be a perfect opportunity to research common North American birds. Consult the *National Audubon Society Field Guide to North American Birds* or Peterson Field Guide series for your location. If you are a bird enthusiast yourself, share your personal experiences and observations with your students. This would make a difference in their motivation and involvement in this project. Ask each student to research a bird, its habitat and nesting patterns, coloration and other interesting facts (including, if possible, a picture or drawing of the bird). Ask students to do an oral presentation of their research. Compile the bird information in a class book. Your finished research and book compilation may become a valuable reference book to your school library.

For a culminating activity, invite parent volunteers on a birdwatching field trip to identify and chart the variety of birds in your community. Further this study by constructing a bird feeder or station near your classroom area for students to observe bird visitations during free times. Have binoculars, books and a chart available for documentation.

For younger students, this could be a class project that they record on a flip chart. They could display the book and resource materials on a table along with student-found items: bird nests, broken egg shells, feathers, etc. Together as a group, look up information and have students write it on the chart. Consider having one bird picture and name per piece of chart paper. The finished project could be bound into a classroom big book.

Categorizing

After reading the story of Bartholomew Cubbins, brainstorm on chart paper a list of different kinds of hats to wear:

cowboy sailor beret tam baseball top stovepipe derby ski
turban stocking helmet army nurse nun's habit straw

Discuss who would wear each kind of hat. Classify hats into "categories," such as:

Hats worn by children   Hats worn for safety   Occupational hats

Knock It Off game

Enjoy a category game called Knock It Off. To make the game, use the following hat pattern. Make enough copies, on red construction paper, to match the number of different kinds of hats you have listed. Using a black marker, label each hat piece with the name of a kind of hat from your brainstorming list. Laminate the hats for durability and attach a piece of magnetic tape on the back of each.

For category headings, enlarge the hat pattern on white paper, making enough copies to match your categories list. Laminate and attach a magnetic strip on the back of these larger hats as well. Allow students to work in small groups to play this game on a magnetic chalk board, placing the red hats (kinds) under the white hats (category).

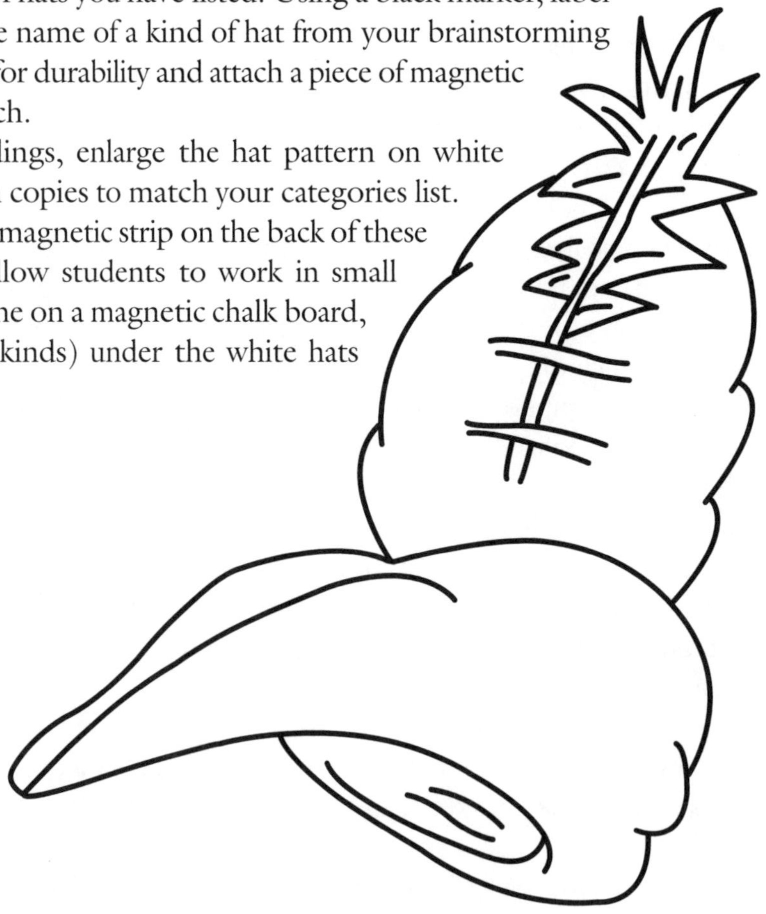

Activity Seventeen

Creative Designing

Bartholomew Cubbins' last 50 hats were all different, the 50th hat being the most unique of all. Encourage your students to participate in preparation for a Hat Parade. Give them a list of supplies and ideas they can use to get started with this assignment:

grocery bags   newspapers   construction paper   feathers   buttons
ribbons   lace   sequins   beads   straw hats

Students can create their own unique hat as a home project or during a specified time during the school day. Consider enlisting the help of your school's art teacher as well.

Hat Parade

Beforehand, schedule a Hat Parade to selected classrooms (or the whole school) to display the finished products. Two children can begin the parade by carrying a banner or sign with the title and author of the book in bold, colorful letters. Another child can carry the Dr. Seuss book up high as the procession marches down the halls and into the classrooms. After the parade is over, take a picture of your students to send to the local newspaper and to put in your classroom photo album. An article in the newspaper can call attention to your author study on Dr. Seuss and the creative imaginations of your students.

 Activity Eighteen

Rainy Day Ideas

Read *The Cat in the Hat* (perhaps on a rainy day), and then ask students what they do on rainy days. Using the example of Sally and her brother, point out to the students that these children didn't watch TV. How could Sally and her brother have entertained themselves if the Cat in the Hat had not appeared? Brainstorm and discuss possible ideas: play cards or board games; work on hobbies — sports cards, stamps, rocks; read a book; call or meet with a friend; paint; have a paper airplane flying contest.

Rainy Day Doings

To motivate and capture students' attention, open an umbrella and display it on a table or suspend it from the ceiling near a bulletin board. Title your bulletin board Rainy Day Doings. Copy and enlarge the raindrop pattern on light blue paper and distribute a sheet for each child to write a rainy day activity on. Allow students to take more than one sheet if they wish. Instruct the children to cut out the completed raindrop and staple it to the bulletin board near the umbrella display. At the end of the day, make time for students to share the ideas they generated.

Some excellent resource books on rainy day ideas are: *52 Things for Your Kids to Do* by Phil Phillips (Nashville, TN: Thomas Nelson, 1992), *A Mother's Manual for Summer Survival* (Colorado Springs, CO: Focus on the Family) and *A Mother's Manual for School Survival* (Colorado Springs, CO: Focus on the Family) by Kathy Peel and Joy Mahaffey.

Raindrop

Cat in the Hat hat

If this activity happens to fall on a rainy day, students might enjoy making a Cat in the Hat hat from construction paper. Use 12"x 18" construction paper and give children a choice of colors with which to design their hat. Each child needs one solid 12"x 18" sheet of construction paper on which to glue other colored strips. *(See pattern on the next page.)* Students then measure their head and staple or glue the paper into a cylinder. Tape the brim and crown to each end of the cylinder hat. Gather your students together for a *Cat in the Hat* class picture. Add the picture to your bulletin board display or class photo album.

Hat pattern

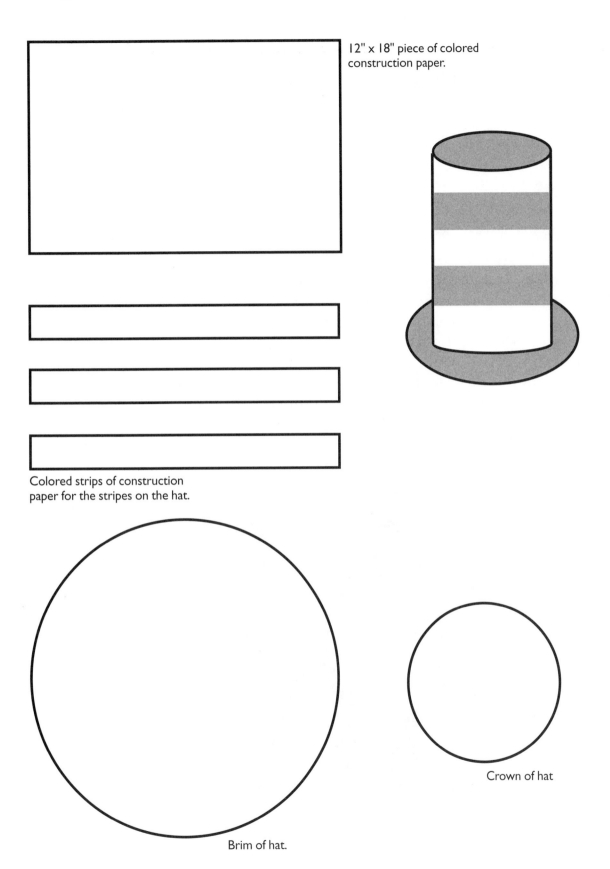

12" x 18" piece of colored construction paper.

Colored strips of construction paper for the stripes on the hat.

Crown of hat

Brim of hat.

Story Starters

Using *The Cat in the Hat* as a springboard, ask students to brainstorm other rhyming couplets to create their own stories. List the story starter ideas on chart paper:

gnat on a bat   mole in a hole   dog on a log   kitten in a mitten
frog in the bog   bear on a chair   fox in a box   fish in a dish

List at least enough couplets to match the number of students in your classroom. Cut the chart paper into strips with one story starter idea on each strip. Ask students to help fold each strip into fourths and place it inside a *Cat in the Hat* hat. Shake the hat to mix up the strips and have each student pull a strip from the hat. This will then be the story starter about which they will write. Keep it a fun, non-threatening activity as students write a short story to share with the class.

Consider expanding this *Cat in the Hat* activity by suggesting students take a picture of their pet cat from home with the *Cat in the Hat* hat on. Encourage them to bring the picture for the bulletin board display.

Activity Twenty

Charades

After reading about Gerald McGrew's new idea for a zoo, ask children what improvements they would make if they could run a zoo. Brainstorm and chart a list of "ordinary" animals in the zoo, then re-read and list the silly animals Gerald told about. Continue this theme by involving your students in a guessing game (like Charades) called In the Zoo.

In the Zoo game

To make this game, glue pictures of zoo animals on 3"x 5" cards. Place the cards in a shoe box decorated like an animal cage. Cut an opening in the top of the shoe box large enough for a child to reach his or her hand inside. To play the game, choose a child to be the "zookeeper." The zookeeper then picks a card at random from the shoe box cage without letting anyone see it. Give the student a couple of minutes to study the card and prepare his or her actions.

When the "zookeeper" seems ready, the waiting children say:

Zookeeper, Zookeeper, what's the clue?
Let us tell you who's in the zoo!

As the zookeeper acts out the animal actions or noises, the first child to raise her hand and guess the correct animal becomes the new zookeeper.

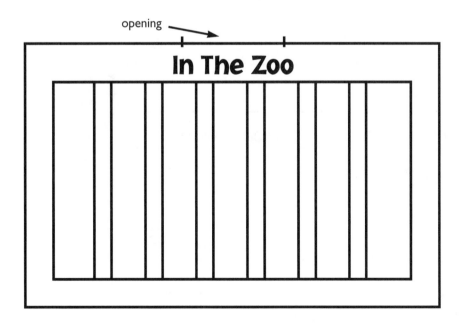

IF/Then Stories

In *If I Ran the Zoo*, Gerald McGrew wanted to change the zoo. Ask your students if they have ever wanted to change how things run. Give them examples, such as:

If I ran the world....   *If I ran the store....*
If I ran the school....   *If I ran the circus....*
Then, what would happen?

Ask your students to brainstorm ideas, pick a topic and write an If... then story (If I ran the _____, then I would _____.) For further background discussion, remind students that Dr. Seuss used regular zoo animals, but their exaggerated names and features. Make sure students list objects, jobs or rules that are standard to the business or job role they want to change, then exaggerate them. For example, if a student chose to write "If I ran the school...," they should list the role of the principal and jobs he or she carries out. The list might look like this:

answers the phone/talks, to important people, types on the computer,
disciplines students, visits classrooms, goes to meetings

Ask students to exaggerate or change the role of the principal to reflect their imagination, such as: "If I ran the school, the answering machine would take all the phone calls." "If I ran the school, students would get a cookie when they were sent to my office." "If I ran the school, I would shut the door and play games on the computer." Students may illustrate their stories and share them with other students or classrooms.

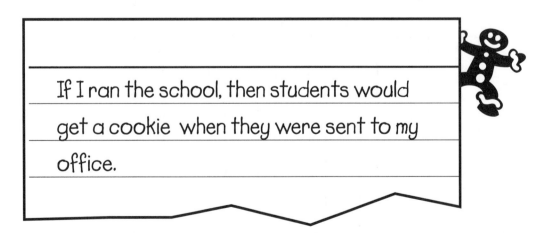

If I ran the school, then students would get a cookie when they were sent to my office.

For additional background, refer to *If I Were in Charge of the World* by Judith Voirst (New York: Macmillan, 1981).

Activity Twenty-Two

Synonyms

After reading Dr. Seuss's books on sleep, brainstorm a list of sleepy time synonyms or synonym phrases with your students. Some examples are:

yawn, dreams, snoring, sleepy, slumber, sleepwalking, cozy bed, drowsy, alarm, asleep, snoozing, counting sheep, bedtime, nighttime, heavy eyelids, tired, lounge, nap, hibernate, doze, nod off, turn in, dreamy, drift off, daydreaming, lethargic, comatose

Ask students to choose a synonym or phrase from the list, write a sentence, short story or poem about it, and illustrate it. Compile the pages together and title it "Sleep Book." Display the finished copy at the Dr. Seuss Center in your classroom.

Snoozy Susy and Tired Ted

For a competitive, culminating activity (possibly for a rainy day), construct two large charts with a sleepy, yawning face illustration. (Possibly ask your school art teacher or artistic student for assistance, or enlarge and use the samples below.) Cut the mouth out. Title the charts "Snoozy Susy" and "Tired Ted." Display the charts on an easel or chart holder, making sure there is free access to the yawning mouth. Using the metal tops off frozen juice cans, press on a white label, and with a black fine tip marker write a sleepy-time synonym or phrase on the label. Make a set of these for each chart. Divide your class into two groups. Instruct each group of students to stand 3' from the Snoozy Susy and Tired Ted charts (mark the distance with a masking tape line).

 Use an alarm clock as a timer. Both groups begin at the same time — each student takes one turn to read the word on the juice lid (with aid if necessary), throw the lid through the mouth of Susy or Ted, and go to the end of the line. If the lid does not go through, the student has to retrieve it for the next student's turn, before going to the end of the line. Play continues until the timer goes off, no matter how often the student has gone through the line. The winning team has the most juice lids piled up on the other side of the chart.

Literature Links

If you wish to continue with the theme of sleep, the following folk and fairy tales may be useful: *Sleeping Beauty, Goldilocks and the Three Bears, The Bremen Town Musicians, Little Red Riding Hood, The Princess and the Pea, Peter Pan, Rip Van Winkle*.

Ask your students if they have favorite bedtime animals (or used to) or certain routines they follow as they get ready for bed. Discuss your bedtime routine and why it's important to you.

You may use the following poems as part of your sleep theme: *"Sleeping Sardines"* by Shel Silverstein, from **Where the Sidewalk Ends** (New York: Harper and Row, 1974) and *"I Should Have Stayed in Bed Today"* from **Something Big Has Been Here** (New York: Greenwillow, 1990) and *"My Family's Sleeping Late Today"* also from **Something Big Has Been Here** (New York: Greenwillow, 1990) by Jack Prelutsky.

My Teddy Bear
I love my little Teddy Bear.
He sleeps with me each night.
And when I turn the light off
I hold him, oh, so tight.

For if I am a bit afraid
And shiver in my fear
My Teddy whispers softly
Sweet nothings in my ear.

Activity Twenty-Four

Author's Purpose

Dr. Seuss wrote *The Butter Battle Book* in 1984 when he was 80 years old. The story describes a heated dispute between the Zooks, who eat their bread with the butter side down, and the Yooks, who eat it with the butter side up. Each country had their own set of habits and beliefs. It seems they could not tolerate each other's differences. Finally, the characters confront each other with bombs in hand. The reader is left wondering who will be the first to drop the bomb.

The author's purpose is to make clear that disagreements and conflicts occur between countries, towns and families as part of life. Some issues are more important than others, but big or small issues must be resolved . . . either through peaceful negotiations or complete destruction. The choice is ours.

This theme could easily launch your students into a discussion on cultural diversity and respect for individual difference in your own classroom community.

Activity Twenty-Five

Conflict Resolution

Ask students to list conflicts that do or could occur in their classroom and how to solve them. Try using the following suggestions as a starting point:

Conflicts
1. Stealing or cheating
2. Pushing and shoving
3. Lying, gossiping, or tattling
4. Fighting
5. Putting down or insulting

Resolutions
1. Confrontation, return of stolen property, apologize.
2. Count to 10 or 20, take a deep breath, think before reacting.
3. Take turns telling each side of the story or problem.
4. Have another person you both respect help in settling the problem.
5. Make a joke about the situation, have a sense of humor.
6. Ignore it or walk away.

Problem Solving

Discuss weapons that have been used down through the ages (slingshot, bow and arrow, catapult, grenade, gun, bomb, etc.) highlighting the ones that resemble Dr. Seuss's crazy creations. Then list the weapons found in *The Butter Battle Book*:

Snick-Berry Switch   Slingshot   Triple-sling Jigger   Jigger-Rock Snatchem
Kick-a-Poo Kid   8-Nozzled, Elephant-Toted Boom Blitz   Yook Utterly Sputter
Zook Utterly Sputter   Yook Bitsy Big-Boy Boomeroo
Zook Bitsy Big-Boy Boomeroo

Divide the class into five groups. Ask each group to design and draw one of the weapons in the story. When finished, ask students to arrange the weapons in the order they were introduced in the story, or from the smallest weapon to the largest.

Leaving this topic on a final, positive note, ask you students to rewrite the story ending so the conflict resolves on peaceful terms. How could the Yooks and Zooks make up? Rather than using weapons that cause bodily injury, could the creatures have invented silly weapons? Keeping your five groups intact, ask your students to come up with alternative weapons that would not harm or injure, such as:

Snick-Berry Tickler   Sling Jigger Feather Puffer
8-Nozzled Water Sprayer   Kick-a-Poo Pillow Pad

Other recommended books about this time period and topic are: *A Present for Prince Paul* (New York: Child's Play, 1995) and *The Prince Who Wrote a Letter* (New York: Child's Play, 1995) both by Ann Love.

Ranking

After reading *The King's Stilts*, discuss King Birtram's favorite pastime activity. Ask your students to think of an activity they like as well as King Birtram liked stilt-walking. Brainstorm a list of pastimes on chart paper. Take a class vote on the most popular of the listed activities and rank them in order of class preference. Design a bulletin board with a pair of red stilts in the center. Write the rank ordered activities on a sentence strip or cut up your brainstorm chart into strips. Then staple the list between the red stilts on your bulletin board. Have students bring photos of themselves or magazine pictures of people enjoying these activities. Place them around the bulletin board.

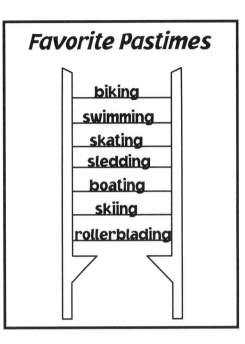

Making stilts

For a culminating activity, ask students to bring in stilts or pogo sticks to experiment with on the playground. You may also wish to make some simple stilts using cans and rope. Ask students, cafeteria workers or parents to save cans for this project. Tall cans (54 oz.) from Grandma Brown's baked beans or family-size (26 oz.) Campbell soup cans work especially well. Using a nail to make a hole in each side of the can, insert a rope (about 2 yds. long) through the holes and tie into a knot. Adjust the length of the rope to fit when standing on the cans. Pull up on the rope firmly to keep the cans on your feet while walking. This activity will give students an idea of how stilt-walking feels.

Natural enemies

In this story, cats were treated with special care. The safety of the entire island depended on how well these cats could keep the Nizzards from pecking at the Dike trees. As we all know, the bird's natural enemy is the cat. What other animals could Dr. Seuss have chosen? If we were to rewrite the story of *The King's Stilts*, discuss how different animals could change the elements and outcome of the story. List animals that are natural enemies:

>   dog/cat   cat/mouse or mole   fox/rabbit   bird/bug or worm

Opposites & Gender Titles

It is interesting to note, of all the books Dr. Seuss wrote in the medieval period, he never included a queen. Display *The Butter Battle Book*, *The 500 Hats of Bartholomew Cubbins*, and *Bartholomew and the Oobleck* for students to find story characters. Ask them to brainstorm a list of male and female medieval royal titles:

King/Queen   Prince/Princess   Emperor/Empress
Lord/Lady   Sorcerer/ Sorceress   Servant/Maid

Discuss how Dr. Seuss's story could have been different if he had included a queen or other royal figures. Have students write their own story including a king and a queen.

Try discussing other gender titles that are clearly male and female, such as those below:

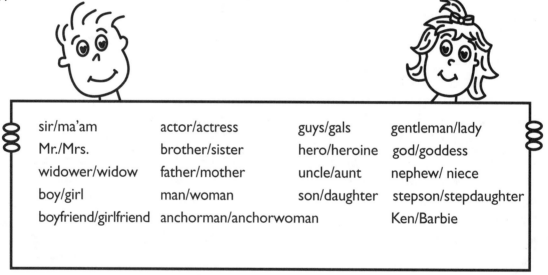

sir/ma'am	actor/actress	guys/gals	gentleman/lady
Mr./Mrs.	brother/sister	hero/heroine	god/goddess
widower/widow	father/mother	uncle/aunt	nephew/ niece
boy/girl	man/woman	son/daughter	stepson/stepdaughter
boyfriend/girlfriend	anchorman/anchorwoman		Ken/Barbie

Specific male and female animal names are:

rooster/hen	bull/cow	ram/ewe	billy goat/nanny goat
buck/doe	gander/goose	boar/sow	lion/lioness
tiger/tigress	stallion/mare		

Consider occupational titles that have changed to accommodate male or female roles, such as:

chairman/chair   fireman/firefighter

Can you list others?

Fantasy vs Reality

After reading *McElligot's Pool*, ask your students if they have any "fish" stories, "big whoppers," or "the-one-that-got-away" stories. Allow time for students to share these stories orally. Or, challenge your students to write a fish story or poem, real or fantasy, by using some of their experiences and/or ideas from Dr. Seuss books and other literature. Discuss the variety of fish from Dr. Seuss's book for background ideas: Fish of any and all types, shapes, colors and sizes.

Sort-a-Fish game

Make the Sort-a-Fish game by tracing three different sizes of fish— small, medium and large—on manilla paper. Label each fish cutout with a fish name. Students may wish to color the fish accurately using pictures for verification. Throw in some of Dr. Seuss's imaginative fish for variety (samples below) and you have a fun sorting game for reality and fantasy, as well as three categories of fish appropriate to your regional area. Use this sorting game along with books on fish for a learning center with two to four students.

Create Sort-a-Fish fantasy fish in three sizes. Use and modify the patterns below or have students create and color their own fish creations to help stock your sorting center.

Classifying kinds of fish

Consider carrying this theme further by researching the kinds of fish found in an aquarium, ocean or lake/stream. If you have a tropical fish tank in your classroom, it may be a helpful source of information to this study. Divide chart paper into three sections. Brainstorm and list fish that would match each topic:

aquarium (Tropical)	*Streams/ponds/lakes* (Fresh water)	*Ocean* (Salt water)
guppy	bass	whale
goldfish	trout	shark
molly	salmon	tuna
angel fish	perch	dolphin
silver hatchet fish	bullhead	barracuda
butterfly fish	pike	sailfish
black moon	sunfish	herring
cory catfish	crappie	cod
blueberry tetra	bluegill	mackerel
striped raphael	carp	manta ray
silver dollar		sawfish
tiger barb		
pink kissing fish		
leaf fish		
red oscar		
Blue zebra		

For additional reading

Make available other literature on the topic of fish and fishing, such as: *"Silver Fish"* from **Where the Sidewalk Ends** by Shel Silverstein (New York: Harper & Row, 1974), **Three Wishes** by Charles Perrault (Mahwah, NJ: Troll, 1979), and *"I Am Sitting Here and Fishing"* from **Something Big Has Been Here** by Jack Prelutsky (New York: Greenwillow, 1990).

Consider copying the poems on the next page on chart paper for display. Perhaps you can have students discuss how the view points of these characters differ from that of Marco.

Everything's Okay
by Cheryl Potts

I went to the river just the other day.
Thought I'd fish, to pass the time away.
I caught my line up in the tree,
But I'm still living,
so everything's okay.

Bill Higby

I tripped on a rock,
dropped my pole,
Spilled my worms and
stubbed my toe.
I sat down slowly,
determined to stay.
But I'm still living, so
everything's okay.

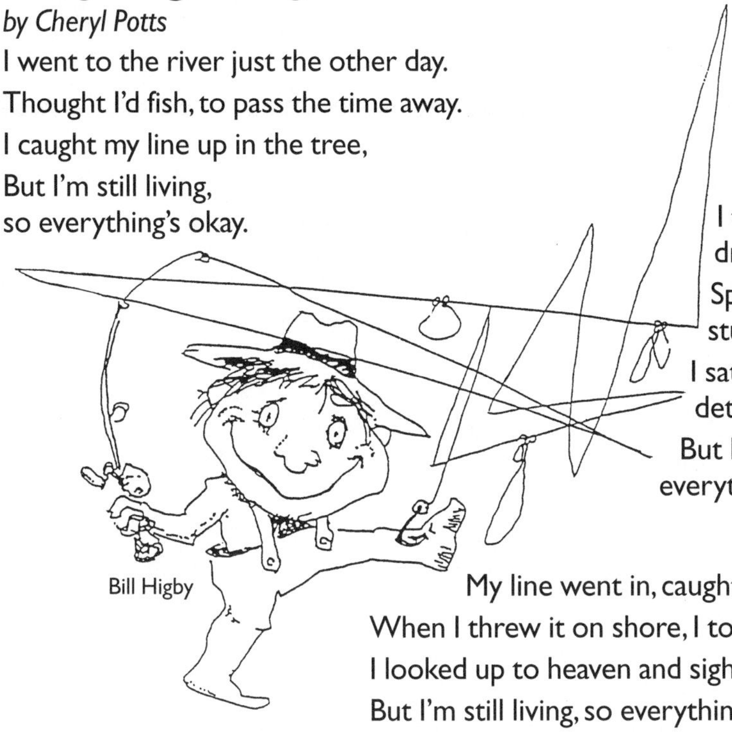

My line went in, caught a fish.
When I threw it on shore, I totally missed.
I looked up to heaven and sighed, "What a day!"
But I'm still living, so everything's okay.

Down by the River's Edge
by Cheryl Potts

Down by the river's edge
Where the frogs jump high,
The toads catch flies,
The birds swoop down,
And turtles lie around.

Down by the river's edge
Where the flowers smell great,
The ferns grow straight,
The snakes slither by,
The bugs just fly.

Down by the river's edge
Where the fish don't bite,
Mosquitos just might,
Where the day is done,
And I haven't caught one.

Down by the river's edge...

Bill Higby

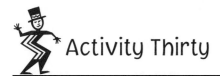 Activity Thirty

Personality Traits

After reading *McElligot's Pool,* notice how Marco is described as a patient child. Not many youngsters would wait three hours to catch a fish. Discuss other positive personality traits that Marco seems to display:

politeness self-control honesty humility confidence persistence
imagination determination

Marco demonstrates these traits in the story:

Politeness and honesty   "It may be you're right...there might be no fish..."

Confidence   "But again, well, there might!"

Persistence.   "This pool might be bigger than you or I know!"

Imagination   "This pool MIGHT be a pool...connected to one of those underground brooks!"

Determination   "...and that's why I think that I'm not such a fool..."

Personality portrait

Using the following picture page, ask your students to draw a picture of their features and hair in place of Marco's. Using the fish pattern from Activity 29, ask students to choose one fish, and write a positive personality trait on it. Have them color and cut out the fish, gluing it to the end of the fish pole on p. 53. Students may color their personality portrait and display the finished pictures in the classroom. Discuss the descriptors students used.

McElligot's Pool
by Dr. Seuss

Cause and Effect

After reading *Bartholomew and the Oobleck,* brainstorm on chart paper a list of words associated with weather. Give opportunities for students to write the words on the chart (Some kindergarten students can write the first letter or two and ending letters.). Some possible words are:

snow rain hail sleet tornado cyclone hurricane sunny hot cloudy fog smog misty lightning thunderstorm windy drizzle blizzard breezy earthquake

Oobleck and other weather conditions

For older students, discuss the cause and effect of the oobleck created by the magicians. Then, ask your students to choose a weather condition that can be researched for its causes and effects, such as: cyclone, tornado, hurricane, earthquake, volcano, hail, lightning, etc. Plan a time for students to share their findings with the class. Compile the information into a book for classroom reference. Title your weather-related book "Oobleck and Other Weather Conditions."

Ask younger students to name and illustrate a weather condition of their choice. On the reverse side of the page, ask each to create something different that could come out of the sky—either something for the good of humanity or something silly. Get the students started by reading *Cloudy With a Chance of Meatballs* by Judi Barrett (New York: Atheneum, 1978).

Discussion and illustrations could also accompany a study on common weather conditions associated with the four seasons: spring, summer, winter, and fall. Ask students to fold a piece of paper into fourths. Open it up and label each section with a season. Ask students to illustrate weather conditions for each season.

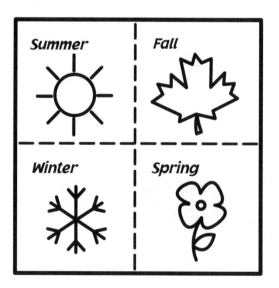

Imagination

Image That! has students complete open-ended statements in a quick brain-storming activity. To prepare, copy and cut out the cloud pattern below. Label and laminate the clouds with the following open-ended statements:

If I were the magician in the story, I would have made....

I like snow because....

One morning, I looked outside and there on the ground was....

If I were Bartholomew Cubbins, I would have told the King....

Instead of rain, I would rather have....

One night, lightning struck a tree and....

It rained so hard, my dad's car....

For the snow sculpture contest, I made a ....

During a terrible storm, the hailstones were as big as....

Suddenly, the cyclone picked up a ....

The fog was so thick, I couldn't ....

The sun was so hot that....

The King could have wished for....

Each time a snowflake landed, it turned into a(n) ....

All of a sudden, the sky grew dark and ....

To play Imagine That!, pass out a cloud to each student or let them draw from several in your hand. Ask them to read it silently and think about how they would finish the statement. Allow students about five minutes or less to quietly brain-storm. Ask for volunteers to read their cloud orally and add their own words to finish it. You may wish to give students the option to pass. This activity could also be turned into a writing project. Collect the stories and make a booklet for students to share with each other.

"I want to learn about..."

Dr. Seuss's book, *I Can Read With My Eyes Shut!* is a great book to start the new school year. Consider decorating your fall bulletin board with *The Cat in the Hat* story character as well as displaying other Dr. Seuss books and posters. If you have a felt *Cat in the Hat* hat, wear it as you read the book to your class. After finishing the story, ask students to brainstorm and list things they would like to learn about this year. Divide the chart into sections, such as: people, animals, places and things. Or, you may want to list items alphabetically. Make a chart with each alphabet letter written down the side, with large enough spaces for students to write their ideas. Leave these charts in an accessible place for students to add ideas throughout the days and weeks of school. After covering topics, cross them off the chart. Use these charts as springboards for student research projects or extra credit reports throughout the school year. At the end of the year, look at the list and discuss the topics of interest covered, either individually or as a group. The purpose of involving students in the topics of learning is to motivate them to read independently.

During the first full week of school, distribute a folder to each student. Ask them to design a cover and title it "Books I've Read." Fill the folder with book charts to log titles each student reads for each month. Use the form on the following page.

Name _____

Books I've Read for the month of_____

	Title	Author
1.		
2.		
3.		
4.		
5.		
6.		
7.		
8.		
9.		
10.		

Books I've Read for the month of_____

	Title	Author
1.		
2.		
3.		
4.		
5.		
6.		
7.		
8.		
9.		
10.		

Activity Thirty-Four

Arts and Crafts

During the last two to three months of school, ask students to choose a favorite book from those read throughout the year. Students will then design a quilt square about the part of the story they liked the best. Using the Favorite Book Quilt sheet *(on the next page)*, ask students to illustrate in pencil inside the dotted square. When the student is completely satisfied, lay precut white fabric on top of the sheet, tape in place and trace the penciled drawing with fabric paint or markers. Be sure to let the paint dry for a day before removing the fabric from the sheet. Make sure students add their name to the square as well as the book title and author.

Enlist the help of a parent volunteer or teacher aide to sew the quilt pieces together. Add loops at the top of the quilt for a dowel to make a classroom wall hanging. This quilt makes a wonderful display in the classroom, library or hallway.

Consider raffling the quilt, using the proceeds for a classroom party or classroom materials. Other ideas include donating it to a local nursing care facility, a public library or as a gift to the principal.

Consider making the quilt squares into a classroom tablecloth, personal apron, skirt and vest, jumper or dress, as a tribute to your students. They will love to see their teacher wear creative and unique items they helped to design.

Favorite Book Quilt

Design your quilt square inside the dotted square. Please include your name, book title and author.

Culminating Activities

- Make a word search or crossword puzzle using the characters of Dr. Seuss's books.

- Select quotations from the various Dr. Seuss books and ask students to match the quotations with the characters who said them.

- Prepare sentences that reflect the main ideas or events from a particular book. Your students will then arrange scrambled story sentences in sequential order.

- Choose one or more of the Dr. Seuss books and complete any of the following activities:

  1. Decide which character in which book you would most like to spend the day with and why.

  2. Choose the book you like most and convince us why we should also.

  3. Compare two of these books. Discuss ways they are alike and ways they are different.

- Choose one of your favorite Dr. Seuss characters and write a riddle about the character for a classmate to guess.

- Make a special Dr. Seuss photo album for displaying pictures of completed projects, plays, drawings, etc., that you accumulated throughout your Dr. Seuss author study.

Dr. Seuss Bibliography

And to Think That I Saw It on Mulberry Street. New York: Vanguard Press, 1937.

The 500 Hats of Bartholomew Cubbins. New York: Vanguard Press, [1937].

The King's Stilts. New York: Random House, [1939].

Horton Hatches the Egg. New York: Random House, [1940].

McElligot's Pool. New York: Random House, [1947].

Thidwick the Big-Hearted Moose. New York: Random House, [1948].

Bartholomew and the Oobleck. New York: Random House, [1949].

If I Ran the Zoo. New York: Random House, [1950].

Scrambled Eggs Super! New York: Random House, [1953].

Horton Hears a Who! New York: Random House, [1954].

On Beyond Zebra. New York: Random House, [1955].

If I Ran the Circus. New York: Random House, [1956].

How the Grinch Stole Christmas! New York: Random House, [1957].

Yertle the Turtle and Other Stories. New York: Random House, [1958].

Happy Birthday to You! New York: Random House, [1959].

The Sneetches & Other Stories. New York: Random House, 1961.

Dr. Seuss's Sleep Book. New York: Random House, [1962].

I Had Trouble in Getting to Solla Sollew. London: Collins, 1965.

I Can Lick 30 Tigers Today! And Other Stories. New York: Random House, [1969].

Did I Ever Tell You How Lucky You Are? New York: Random House, [1973].

Dr. Seuss Storytime. New York: Random House, [1974].

The Lorax. New York: Random House, [1971].

Hunches in Bunches. New York: Random House, 1982.

The Butter Battle Book. New York: Random House, 1984.

You're Only Old Once! New York: Random House, 1986.

Oh, the Places You'll Go! New York: Random House, 1990.

Daisy-Head Mayzie. New York: Random House, 1994.

My Many Colored Days. Illustrated by Steve Johnson with Lou Fancher. New York: Knopf ; distributed by Random House, 1996.

What Was I Scared Of? New York: Random House, 1997.

Beginning Readers

The Cat in the Hat. Boston: Houghton Mifflin, [1957].

The Cat in the Hat Comes Back. New York: Beginner Books, [1958]

One Fish Two Fish Red Fish Blue Fish. New York: Beginner Books; distributed by Random House, c1960.

Green Eggs and Ham. New York: Beginner Books, 1960.

Hop on Pop. New York: Beginner Books, 1963.

Dr. Seuss's ABC. New York: Beginner Books, 1963.

The Cat in the Hat Dictionary by the Cat himself and P. D. Eastman. New York: Beginner Books, [1964].

Fox in Socks. New York: Beginner Books, [1965].

The Foot Book. New York: Random House, [1968].

My Book About Me, by Me, Myself. I Wrote It! I Drew It! With a little help from my friends Dr. Seuss and Roy McKie. New York: Beginner Books, [1969]

Mr. Brown Can Moo! Can You? New York: Random House, [1970].

I Can Draw It Myself, by Me, Myself. New York: Beginner Books, [1970].

Marvin K. Mooney, Will You Please Go Now! New York: Random House, [1972].

The Shape of Me and Other Stuff. New York: Beginner Books, [1973].

There's a Wocket in My Pocket! New York: Beginner Books, [1974].

Great Day for Up! Pictures by Quentin Blake. New York: Beginner Books, [1974].

Wacky Wednesday. Illus. by George Booth. New York: Beginner Books, [1974].

Oh, the Thinks You Can Think! New York: Beginner Books, [1975].

Hooper Humperdink--? Not him! Illustrated by James Stevenson. New York: Beginner Books, 1976.

The Cat's Quizzer. New York: Beginner Books, 1976.

I Can Read With My Eyes Shut. New York: Beginner Books, 1978.

Oh Say Can You Say? New York: Beginner Books, 1979.

I Am Not Going to Get Up Today. Illustrated by James Stevenson. New York: Beginner Books, 1987.

About Dr. Seuss

Dr. Seuss Enterprises. *Seuss-isms.* New York: Random House, 1997.

The Grolier Library of North American Biographies. Connecticut: Grolier Educational Corporation, 1994.

Morgan, Judith & Neil. *Dr. Seuss & Mr. Geisel.* New York: Random House, 1995.

San Diego Museum of Art. *Dr. Seuss From Then to Now.* New York: Random House, 1986.

Wheeler, Jill. *Dr. Seuss.* Minnesota: Abdo & Daughters, 1992.

Teacher Resource Books

Baltas, Joyce, ed. *Balanced Reading K–2*. New York: Scholastic Professional Books, 1996.

Chapin, Laurie & Flegenheimer-Riggle, Ellen. *Leaping into Literature*. Columbus, OH: Good Apple, 1990.

Cook, Shirley & Carl, Kathy. *Linking Literature & Writing*. Nashville: Incentive Publications, Inc., 1989.

Daniel, Becky. *Reading Brainstorms*. Columbus, OH: Good Apple, 1990.

Davis, Robin Works. *An Alphabet of Books* and *An Alphabet of Authors*. Fort Atkinson, WI: Alleyside Press, 1994-1996.

Evans, Joy & Moore, Jo Ellen. *How to Make Books With Children*. Monterey, CA: Evan Moor, 1985.

Jenson, Janice. *Literature-Based Learning Activities Kit*. West Nyack, NJ: Center for Applied Research in Education, 1991.

Luetje, Carolyn & Quinn, Carol. *Poem Patterns*. San Juan Capistrano, CA: Edupress, 1988.

Mallett, Jerry. *Reading Bulletin Boards & Display Kit*. West Nyack, NJ: Center for Applied Research in Education, 1988.

Milliken, Linda. *Easy Book Projects*. San Juan Capistrano, CA: Edupress, 1989.

Muncy, Patricia Tyler. *Hooked on Books!* Englewood Cliffs, NJ: Prentice Hall, 1995.

Perry, Phyllis J. *Reading Activities & Resources That Work*. Fort Atkinson, WI: Alleyside Press, 1997.

Philpot, Jan Grubb. *Book-a-Brations!* Nashville: Incentive Publications, 1990.

Richards, Joanne & Standley, Marianne. *One for the Books*. Nashville: Incentive Publications, 1984.

Stafford, E.V. *Launch Into Literature II*. Minneapolis, MN: T.S. Denison, 1990.

Warren, Jean, comp. *Theme-a-Saurus*. Everett, WA: Warren Publishing House, 1989.